A B C

by Stephanie Calmenson
illustrated by John Nez

Featuring Jim Henson's Sesame Street Muppets

A Sesame Street / Golden Press Book
Published by Western Publishing Company, Inc. in conjunction
with Children's Television Workshop.

© 1986 Children's Television Workshop. Sesame Street Muppets © Muppets, Inc. 1986.
All rights reserved. Printed in the U.S.A. by Western Publishing Company, Inc.
No part of this book may be reproduced or copied in any form without written
permission from the publisher. Sesame Street® and the Sesame Street sign are
trademarks and service marks of Children's Television Workshop. GOLDEN®,
GOLDEN & DESIGN®, A GOLDEN TELL-A-TALE® BOOK, and GOLDEN PRESS® are
trademarks of Western Publishing Company, Inc. Library of Congress Catalog Card
Number: 85-82185   ISBN 0-307-07016-6   DEFGHIJ

A a airplane

B b

bubble

C c   cookie

D d duck

E e egg

F f firefighter

G g guitar

I i ice cream

J j

jack-in-the-box

K k kite

L l leaf

M m monster

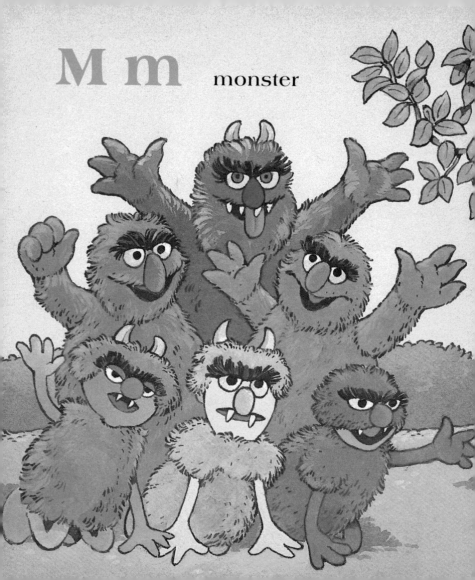

N n   nest

O o octopus

Q q queen

R r rabbit

S s saw

T t telephone

U u   umbrella

V v valentine

W W witch

X x x ray

Y y yo-yo

Z z zebra

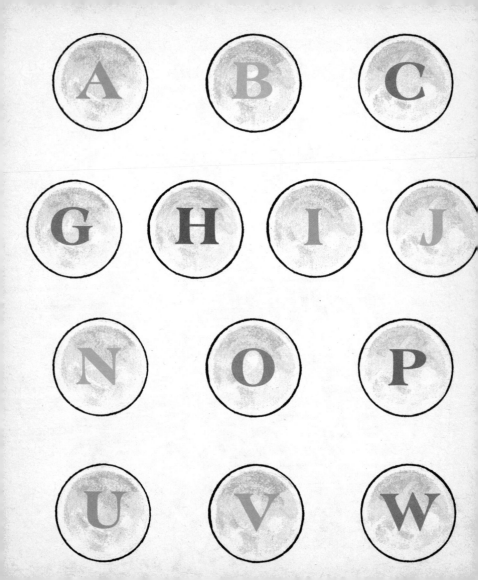